Improvement in 3-D

Book 3

DECISION MAKING
Techniques to Leverage Your B.R.A.I.N. Workbook

Decision Making

Amy K. Atcha

Improvement in 3-D

Book 3

DECISION MAKING
Techniques to Leverage Your B.R.A.I.N. Workbook

Decision Making

Decision Making: Techniques to Leverage Your B.R.A.I.N. Workbook
By: Amy K. Atcha

Cover design by: Wayne Johnson

Published by: Customized Caring Publishing
ISBN – 13: 978-0692217603

For information about special discounts on bulk purchases,
Contact Customized Caring, Inc. at 630.306.4480 or www.customizedcaring.com.

Decision Making

About this Book

The Decision Making: Techniques to Leverage Your B.R.A.I.N. workbook is part of the Improvement in 3-D series. It has been designed to provide you with the opportunity to absorb the concepts, acquire the skills and advance your techniques, taking an active role in creating your leadership style. With Improvement in 3-D, you will learn, grow, and enhance your own delegation, due diligence and decision making abilities, as well as assisting those around you. As you study and strengthen your own skills, you will become more creative, more productive and more successful!

As a person, a group member, and as a leader, the information and questions in these books are designed to get you thinking. The exercises are designed to help you practice and implement new methods, expanding your gallery of techniques in all kinds of ways - personally, professionally, in your family, your work or any organization. You will be amazed as you watch your own skills grow to new heights, right along with those around you. Your attitude and style as a leader will never be the same.

The Improvement in 3-D workbooks are effective tools for learning, assessing, strategizing, and practicing methods and techniques. You can use these books for individual training and development, or with a group, to increase your productivity.

The information, tools and tips in these books will stay with you (and your organization) long after you finish the series. Use the guidance, structures and approaches over and over.

Are you ready to start? It's time for Improvement in 3-D!

Decision Making

Techniques to Leverage Your B.R.A.I.N. Workbook

Contents

Decision Making

Preface

Whether it's your first day on the job, your 20th year of helping out an organization, or you just need a bit more personal development in your life, it's never too soon (or too often!) for Improvement.

Improvement comes in many forms – mental, physical, structural and systematic – just to name a few.   It can be achieved individually, in a group, and even as an organization. The great learners and scholars, along with entrepreneurs and businesspeople, never stop improving on themselves, their products, their thinking and their companies.

With each step that you take, you will grow, <u>and</u> seek out even more ways to improve. Soon, you will conceptualize, then visualize, strategize and formulate, and finally implement ways for Improvement.

The third of this three part series on Improvement is on Decision Making. It may be considered a stand-alone segment or a step on your journey to improve. Either way, it will continue your thinking, planning and working in a more productive and successful manner.

Whether you are new to decision making, or have already made several complex, multi-faceted, long-range decisions that affect hundreds of people, you can agree with Mary Doria Russell when she said, "The sign of a good decision is the multiplicity of reasons for it."

Or perhaps this statement by Malcom Gladwell better fits your beliefs, "Truly successful decision-making relies on a balance between deliberate and instinctive thinking."

Thinking in 3-D conjures up many images – many dimensions – of the same, yet different, perspectives. When we think 3-D, we create a structure in our minds that references length, width and depth. In terms of working and creating, we may operate in 3-D:

> 1-D: doing it your way

> 2-D: asking others how they do it

> **3-D: working together to create a GREAT process, a GREAT product, a GREAT team**

The same goes for our Delegation, our Due Diligence and our Decision Making.

> Delegation – up, down and across

> Due Diligence from a variety of sources

> Decision Making, not just at one level, but considering other factors includes resources (time, money, people), style and method.

Throughout your work in this Improvement in 3-D Series, practice thinking in all three capacities, work on different levels and with different perspectives, and build on your success through knowledge, training and result!

The sections of this book will provide you with basic information and guidance about the concept and reasoning behind decision making, as well as the steps and instructions for some of the best approaches to decision making. At the back are Tools you can use to begin (or enhance) your decision making skills.

DECISION MAKING and your B.R.A.I.N. gives you the context in which we will use Decision Making for this book.

Breaking It Down describes the various perspectives and styles used to make decisions. Here we will also discuss the ABCD's of decision making, and Why complex decision making skills are so important. This section takes you step by step through the various aspects of the process, along with providing you useful techniques and exercises to move you towards more decisive, intentional action.

Mastering the Decision lets you practice the skills by trying out the techniques with simulations and scenarios.

Helpful Tools are resources provided for future study, practice and use.

It's time to Use Your B.R.A.I.N.! is your call to action!

Now is the time to absorb the knowledge.

Now is the time to enhance your abilities.

Now is the time to leverage your leadership potential.

Now is the time for Improvement in 3-D!

Decision Making

DECISION MAKING and Your B.R.A.I.N.

Decision making is "the thought process of selecting a logical choice from the available options," according to the Business Dictionary. The Dictionary further states, "for effective decision making, a person must be able to forecast the outcome of each option as well, and based on all these items determine which option is the best for that particular situation."

We make a myriad of decisions every day. Some decisions are routine, easy, and done almost without any thought. Other decisions are elaborate, complex, and strategic, with life changing social, financial, and corporate ramifications.

So how is it that we make such wonderful – or disastrous – decisions? Do we think, research, plan then implement? Or are we simply reacting to an occasion or chain of events that is thrust upon us with no warning?

Do we take, or even have, the time to fully analyze what alternatives exist and what the consequences of our decisions will be?

The answer to these questions is yes . . . and no . . . sometimes . . . maybe . . . it depends.

The starting point for any decision is straight forward – use your B.R.A.I.N.

By using your B.R.A.I.N., you will incorporate the process of slowing down your thoughts, giving yourself, and others involved a chance to fully appreciate the situation, consider options, and strategize. Then, once a decision has been made, you can feel confident that your actions will play out with success.

Leaders make hundreds of decisions every week. Their decisions affect the lives of their employees, their followers, and themselves. Leaders need, and want, to ensure that they are making the best decisions for the matters at hand. They must think before they act.

Great leaders do not make decisions, at least those that are significant, on a whim. Great leaders follow a process in their decision making. Great leaders use their B.R.A.I.N. (some, without even knowing it!)!

Since Decision Making and its association with Leadership can mean different things to different people, let's start with a brief discussion and exercise.

Decision Making

Decision Making is the cognitive process of reaching a decision. We make a multitude of decisions, big and small, every day.

When I think of Decision Making, I think of:

1.

2.

3.

Leadership

Leadership has many characteristics. We tend to think of Leaders as managers, bosses or superiors. We think of a Leader as the person who is responsible for "getting the job done".

What is leadership?

1.

2.

3.

Now, let's combine the two concepts.

List individuals (leaders) that make decisions.

1.

2.

3.

4.

5.

6.

7.

8.

9.

10.

Your B.R.A.I.N.

We use our brains, in more ways than one, to help make decisions – especially those that are complex. Or, at least we should be. We use the knowledge we have gained, our previous experiences, our opinions, and our values. We actually do, physically speaking, process decisions using our brains.

But your B.R.A.I.N. means so much more!

You can also use your B.R.A.I.N. to provide a structure or format to the process of decision making. B.R.A.I.N. is an acronym:

<u>B</u>enefits
<u>R</u>isks
<u>A</u>lternatives
<u>I</u>ntuition
<u>N</u>othing

And since we are using our B.R.A.I.N.s, let's not forget that virtually everything we do involves components of research, training, and being goal-oriented. Let's cover some basics, then we'll break it down and explore some more.

Benefits

There are benefits to any decision we make. But not all benefits have to be tangible, or economic or even company oriented.

What are possible Benefits to a decision?

1.

2.

3.

Risks

Similarly, there are risks to any decision we make. Not all risks are devastating however. Not all risks are financial in nature either.

What are possible Risks to a decision?

1.

2.

3.

Alternatives

For each decision we need to make, several alternatives exist.

What are possible Alternatives to a decision?

1.

2.

3.

Intuition

Your intuition or your "gut" can tell you a lot about a decision.

What does using your Intuition mean?

1.

2.

3.

Nothing

For some decisions, doing nothing is an option.

What does doing Nothing mean? How is it a choice?

1.

2.

3.

Research

Almost every aspect of Decision Making involves doing research. This gathering of information can be viewed in several ways from very specific details to broader knowledge.

When I think of Research, I think of:

1.

2.

3.

Areas of Research needed in Decision Making:

1.

2.

3.

Training

Training is involved in everything we do that is new to us. Decision Making will require that we learn new skills. Training is involved whether we are new to the experience, just want professional development or are doing succession planning. Training never ends!

When I think of Training, I think of:

1.

2.

3.

Areas of Training provided through Decision Making:

1.

2.

3.

Goal Oriented

Goals are the outcomes we want or expect from a given assignment, task or project. Goals can be personal or professional, tangible or intangible, specific or general. Thinking broadly, goals can include something as simple as "gaining greater, more varied knowledge of the industry".

When I think of a project or a decision as being goal oriented, I think of:

1.

2.

3.

Goals to be gained from Decision Making include:

1.

2.

3.

Let's practice. Consider one situation: You have several small administrative projects to do, all with due dates before the end of the quarter. Your boss has told you additional resources are available to complete your workload, if you wish. What decisions do you need to make? Fill in the blanks, then let's discuss.

TOO Much Work! – Decision Making

What is the goal I am trying to achieve?

What do I know now?

What additional information do I need?

What constraints or limitations exist?

What are the Benefits to the decision?

What are the Risks to the decision?

What Alternatives exist?

What is my Intuition telling me?

What if I do Nothing?

Is any training needed?

My final decision is . . .

You've just made your first decision using your B.R.A.I.N.!

Don't stop here!

Now that you have the general idea, we'll break it down.   Then we'll head in the other direction, taking it one step further to learn some **Techniques to Leverage Your B.R.A.I.N.!**

Decision Making

Breaking It Down

In this section, we will work on breaking down the Decision Making model. We will discuss the five basic steps to making decisions, as well as various collaborative methods. We will then move to an important, and routinely unappreciated, discussion about other factors that influence our decisions, thus turning even the seemingly easy choice into a complex dilemma and solution. We will end the chapter with a short discussion of the **Keys to Success**.

Basic Steps in Decision Making

There are five basic steps to making any decision.

1. **Define the problem** – Before you can begin to solve your problem, you must know what your problem is. You must identify a goal to your decision making. Keep in mind that your goal may be very specific or broad. If your initial goal is broader, your subsequent goals for the related project may become narrower as decisions are made.

2. **Gather information** – Once you identify your goal, then it is time to gather information. Using your due diligence and delegation skills, obtain all relevant information which will assist you in making a decision. Be sure to be expansive in your thinking at this stage. The more information, the better (within reason).

3. **Generate alternatives** – The third step is to generate viable alternatives. For each possible alternative, list the benefits, the risks and the resulting consequences if the decision were to be acted upon. Sometimes the benefits (and the risks) become apparent only after thinking through the consequences of the action.

4. **Select a choice and implement** – Now that you have your list of possibilities, you must select one <u>and</u> act on it. Prior to your selection, be sure to evaluate each choice using a standard scale or weighting – with all factors considered. Some risks may outweigh the benefits when paired together. Additionally, without acting on your choice, the decision making process will not be fully realized.

5. **Evaluate** – When your decision has been made and executed, it is time to reflect. Evaluate the outcomes – good and bad. Did you accomplish what you wanted? Was your problem resolved? Were there any additional benefits that you did not expect? Were there consequences you had not anticipated? Was your decision a success?

Likely you have heard of a few other variations to the B.R.A.I.N. approach. Use these techniques to leverage your B.R.A.I.N.   Details on these methods are in the Helpful Tools section of this workbook.

<u>Pros and Cons</u>

On opposite sides of the page, list all the positives and negatives to the decision, or to each alternative. Consider the weightings – does one benefit have a greater impact than two risks?   Instead of Pro / Con, use opposing terms such as Risk / Reward and Cost / Benefit

<u>"What if?" scenarios</u>

Working through the various alternatives, what is the likely result(s) of each choice? Map the outcome, level by level, until you reach the final output. Thinking the scenario through to the end might help you determine your initial steps.

<u>The Options Wheel</u>

Identify all possible options, using each "spoke" on the wheel as a different alternative. For each spoke, identify how strongly you feel about the benefit of that option.

Also for each spoke, consider the risk level of the option. Does a visual representation help to make the decision?

<u>The Consequences Chart</u>

For every action, there will be a consequence. Write the anticipated Best Case or Desired result on one end of a continuum, with the corresponding Worst Case result at the other end. Where do think the chosen action / option will fall on the line? Consider the effect each option has on the Company, the Project Team, You, Time, Money and other Resources.

You can plot the various effects in different colors along the lines of each option. Does this visual representation of potential outcomes assist you in making the decision?

Collaborating and Communicating

Overlaying the process of decision making, there are various methods which are used to "work on" and "solve" the problem, aka to Make a Decision. These methods range from the simple do-it-yourself approach, to a much more complex, organizational, collaborative, group structure. It's important to note that no one approach is best for every situation.

There are generally two groups of decision making approaches – those methods where the decision is effectively made by one individual, and those styles done by groups. Of course, each of these two categories can be further broken down.

<u>Individual Decision Making Styles</u>

The Authoritarian approach or **Autocratic** method is very directive. The basis of this scheme is that the group leader solves the problem. Its fast; it's easy. This method works well for rational or logical decisions.

Decisions made by an Autocratic approach include:

1.

2.

3.

Sometimes, however, a leader does not immediately have all the information that is needed to make a decision. During these times, a more **Analytical** approach might be used, with the leader seeking advice from others. Leaders who like to be well-informed use this method. Yet, in the end, the leader remains the one to make the decision.

Decisions made in an Analytical method include:

1.

2.

3.

Finally, another individual type of decision making style is the **Collective** or **Participative** approach. Using this method, the leader involves a team to gather information, and even to evaluate the options and risks, but makes the final decision alone AND is responsible for the outcome – good or bad.

Decisions made using the Collective / Participative approach include:

1.

2.

3.

Group Decision Making Styles

Just as there are several variations to an individual decision making approach, the same holds true with group decision making.

In the **Conceptual** approach, the leader explains the problem / goal to the team and provides it with relevant information. Together, they generate and evaluate solutions. This approach works best from a long-term perspective. Solutions tend to be more creative and expansive.

Decisions made using the Conceptual approach include:

1.

2.

3.

Using a **Behavioral** method, the leader will explain the problem / goal to the team and provide all known information. The team will together reconcile differences among themselves and negotiate a solution that is acceptable to all. In this approach, the leader may also consult other experts to generate additional alternatives. This method is typically used to avoid conflict. It places importance on the acceptance by others.

Decisions made using the Behavioral approach include:

1.

2.

3.

With the **Consensus** approach, the leader gives up control. The team makes the decision, thus being responsible for the outcome. This approach requires that everyone "buy in" to the solution.

Decisions made using the Consensus approach include:

1.

2.

3.

Similar to the previous approach, using a **Democratic** method, the leader also gives up control and the team makes the decision. However, unlike the Consensus approach, not everyone has to agree or "buy in" to the final solution. In the Democratic approach, the group votes and the majority win.

Decisions made using the Democratic approach include:

1.

2.

3.

In a perfect world, decisions would be easy to make. In a very linear fashion, alternatives would be identified, benefits and risks fully appreciated, and the choice relatively simple. Yet, that is not how most decisions are made. Certain **Other Factors** come in to play when any one of us (or even all of us working together!) is making a decision.

These other factors can be divided into various areas based upon the root focus or cause of the underlying perception. The general areas include those that are derived based on individual or personal forces such as internal factors, external factors, the motivation of the decision maker, developmental ability, or other clouding factors.

Internal – focus of control, previous experiences, need for immediate gratification

External – relationships, long term goals, resources (cost, human capital)

Motivational - beliefs, values, attitudes, emotional state, expectations

Developmental - cognitive, affective, social norms, social approval

Clouding - anxiety, fear, anger, drugs

In addition, when taken as whole, other factors can affect the group dynamic of decision making as well. Group problems can arise when there is:

Domination by a few very vocal members

Social pressures

Group think (usually in an effort to avoid conflict)

Other factors that affect my personal decisions include:

1.

2.

3.

4.

5.

Other factors that affect my professional decisions include:

1.

2.

3.

4.

5.

Time is the final factor that can affect any decision. In some situations, time is of the essence – there is no time to wait; an action is required immediately.

In other situations, however, a better, more proper decision may be made only after gathering additional information, waiting for related events to take place, or simply postponing a decision until circumstances change. It is important not to make "knee jerk reaction" decisions, without evaluating the alternatives and the consequences.

For those decisions which do not have an imminent need, jot down your thoughts, the facts, your concerns. Let the questions or problems "simmer" on the back burner. Make the decision when the time is "right", when the time is optimal for the issues at hand.

Situations which require immediate decisions include:

1.

2.

3.

Situations where decisions can be postponed:

1.

2.

3.

Just as it is helpful to identify the various alternatives to a decision, it is also helpful to identify and write down alternatives on how decisions will be made and by whom. Use the following chart, found in the Helpful Tools section to assist you.

<u>Who Decides?</u>

Who will be making the decision? How will you, or your team, be making it? Will you seek guidance from outside experts? Will you analyze and evaluate together as a team? Does your decision need to be unanimous? Who else will be affected? Do these individuals have a vote in the process? Who will lead the communication and announcement of the decision? Writing out your thoughts will help solidify, and justify, your decisions.

As you can see from our discussions, different styles are best used in different circumstances. There is not one fool-proof method or manner to decision making. It takes skill, practice and patience.

Remember too that your decisions do not exist in a vacuum. Get feedback, analyze how the decisions you make affect other people, relationships, and the organization as a whole. Keep in mind that current decisions can, and will, influence future behavior.

Keys to Success

Purpose

To achieve the greatest rewards and have the most positive experiences (i.e. SUCCESS), it is essential to have AND know the purpose behind what and why you are making the decisions you make.   As you work through your project plan (yes, you should PLAN and strategize prior to making a decision) make a note as to the purpose for each part of the process.

Communication/ Collaboration

As with all matters big and small, communication (and most times, collaboration) is key. The method as well as the manner in which information is obtained and disseminated can determine the success of the project. Initially you, and your team, are gathering facts, not creating bias with your own opinions and assumptions. Alternatives should be considered in conjunction with your group or the end users in mind. Work with your team and your client to make and execute the best decisions. Keep RESPECT and OBJECTIVITY at the forefront of any exchanges – written or verbal, individual or group based.

Act with Educated Intent at the Appropriate Time

No one wants, or should, make a "snap" decision. Take time to evaluate your options, considering the costs and the consequences. Then, having done your research, ACT with educated intent. Certain decisions are time-sensitive. If you wait too long to act, your circumstances may change – for better or for worse. The timing of your decisions, and corresponding actions, will help you achieve success.

Patience

We all need to have patience, whether it's at home or at work. Remember, Decision Making can be subjective. Identifying all the benefits, risks and alternatives to any problem does not happen overnight. You will not know exactly where to stop on your first time, your second time, or maybe ever. The key to remember is to learn along the way, and work to improve and enhance your skills through your experiences. For this, you need Patience.

Decision Making

Mastering the Decision

We've talked about Decision Making – what it is, what it involves and why it's important, and even broken it down step by step. We've discussed who makes decisions and how. Now, let's practice.

Following are 3 scenarios. After reading the summary of each, fill in the worksheet that follows.

Scenario One: New Family Room Furniture

It's Spring and time for a change. After sitting in the family room all winter, you've grown bored with the furniture. You realize it's been 8 years since you moved into your house, and the furniture was not new then. The longer you sit, the more you notice how tattered and stained it is. Even the throw pillows are flat and lifeless.

Is it time to get new furniture? How much is it going to cost? Will getting a new couch and love seat also require new pictures, curtains and lamps? Is this a family decision? Or would it be better to just find a new family room set, buy it, and then tell everyone?

The styles, the colors, the selection?! How do you decide? Where do you begin?

Scenario Two: Helping Mom and Dad

Last week, you took a short trip to visit Mom and Dad. It had been several months since you'd last seen them, but something about this visit seems to be bothering you more than usual.

As you reflect for a moment, you realize - Mom and Dad have aged considerably over the past year. Before, they were active and energetic. Now, they seem to be moving slower, forgetting things and generally just seem to need help even doing their daily chores. You had not noticed all this before, but now you can't get it out of your head.

Do they need a caregiver or other support? If so, who? You can't quit your job; your sister lives on the other side of the country. What will you do? How can you help them? And what will Mom and Dad do if something serious were to happen?

Scenario Three: Low Sales Volume

You are the Operations Manager at Fairfax, Inc., a manufacturing firm.   During the most recent 3 months you've noticed that the sales volume has been declining. In fact, year to date the total volume has decreased by 20%, and the "busy season" has already ended. To make matters worse, it seems like costs on some of the raw materials are increasing considerably. Some changes are definitely needed.

Not only do you need to report this to the Board of Directors, but you also need to come up with solutions to rectify, or at least temper, the situation.

 What are your options? What will you tell the Board? And when?   You can always hope that things will improve next quarter, but what if they don't?

SCENARIO ONE: New Family Room Furniture

What is the goal I am trying to achieve?

What do I know now?

What additional information do I need?

What constraints or limitations exist?

What are the Benefits to the decision?

What are the Risks to the decision?

What Alternatives exist?

What is my Intuition telling me?

What if I do Nothing?

Is any training needed?

What are the Pros and Cons of each alternative?

Is there a long term benefit that will outweigh a short term risk?

Who should be making this decision? Me alone?   Others?

What is influencing my decision?

What is my time frame for making the decision?

What is my time frame for acting on the decision?

What, and who, will be impacted as a result of this decision?

Have I considered "What if" scenarios?

How will I evaluate the outcome?

My final decision is . . .

SCENARIO TWO: Helping Mom and Dad

What is the goal I am trying to achieve?

What do I know now?

What additional information do I need?

What constraints or limitations exist?

What are the Benefits to the decision?

What are the Risks to the decision?

What Alternatives exist?

What is my Intuition telling me?

What if I do Nothing?

Is any training needed?

What are the Pros and Cons of each alternative?

Is there a long term benefit that will outweigh a short term risk?

Who should be making this decision? Me alone? Others?

What is influencing my decision?

What is my time frame for making the decision?

What is my time frame for acting on the decision?

What, and who, will be impacted as a result of this decision?

Have I considered "What if" scenarios?

How will I evaluate the outcome?

My final decision is . . .

SCENARIO THREE: Low Sales Volume

What is the goal I am trying to achieve?

What do I know now?

What additional information do I need?

What constraints or limitations exist?

What are the Benefits to the decision?

What are the Risks to the decision?

What Alternatives exist?

What is my Intuition telling me?

What if I do Nothing?

Is any training needed?

What are the Pros and Cons of each alternative?

Is there a long term benefit that will outweigh a short term risk?

Who should be making this decision? Me alone? Others?

What is influencing my decision?

What is my time frame for making the decision?

What is my time frame for acting on the decision?

What, and who, will be impacted as a result of this decision?

Have I considered "What if" scenarios?

How will I evaluate the outcome?

My final decision is . . .

Decision Making

Helpful Tools

Decision Making is not a concrete, rigid process or structure. After all, the Decision Making that is required, and which you may want to make to enhance yourself and your company, will depend on your circumstances, your time frames, your resources, and of course your goals. No two projects will ever be alike!

However, rather than having to "start at square one" each time, the following Helpful Tools have been developed to offer you a framework for creating your next Decision Making scheme.

Basic Outline for Decision Making

What is the goal I am trying to achieve?

What do I know now?

What additional information do I need?

What constraints or limitations exist?

What are the Benefits to the decision?

What are the Risks to the decision?

What Alternatives exist?

What is my Intuition telling me?

What if I do Nothing?

Is any training needed?

My final decision is . . .

<u>**Pro / Con - Risk / Reward - Cost / Benefit**</u>

Problem to Solve: _____

<u>Pro</u> _____   <u>Con</u> _____

<u>Rewards</u> _____   <u>Risks</u> _____

<u>Benefits</u> _____   <u>Costs</u> _____

Decision _____

<u>What IF Scenario Work Flow Form</u>

Date: _____   Project: _____

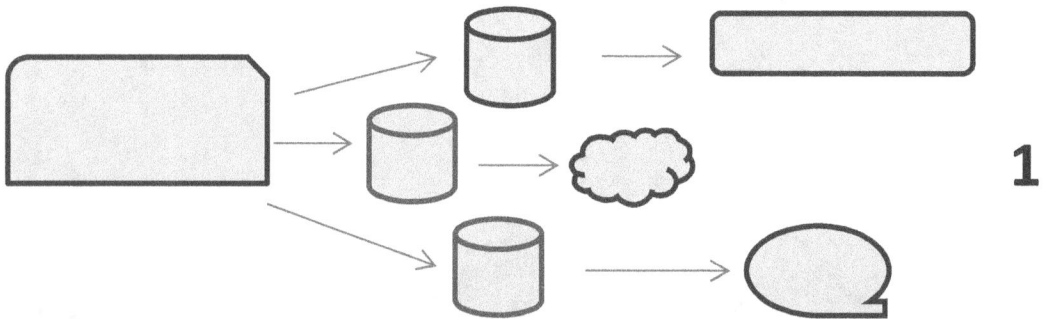

1

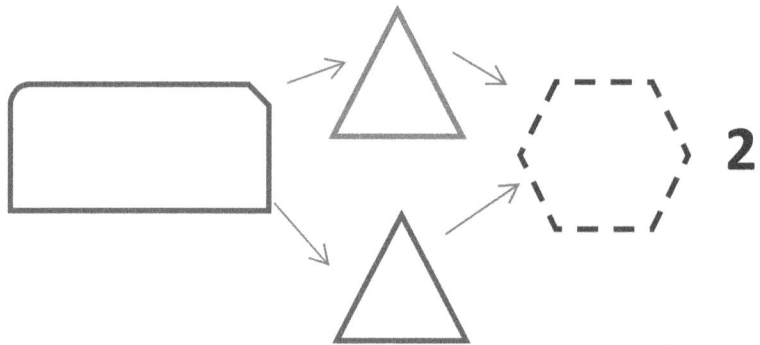

2

3

Options Wheel Form

Decision to be made: _____

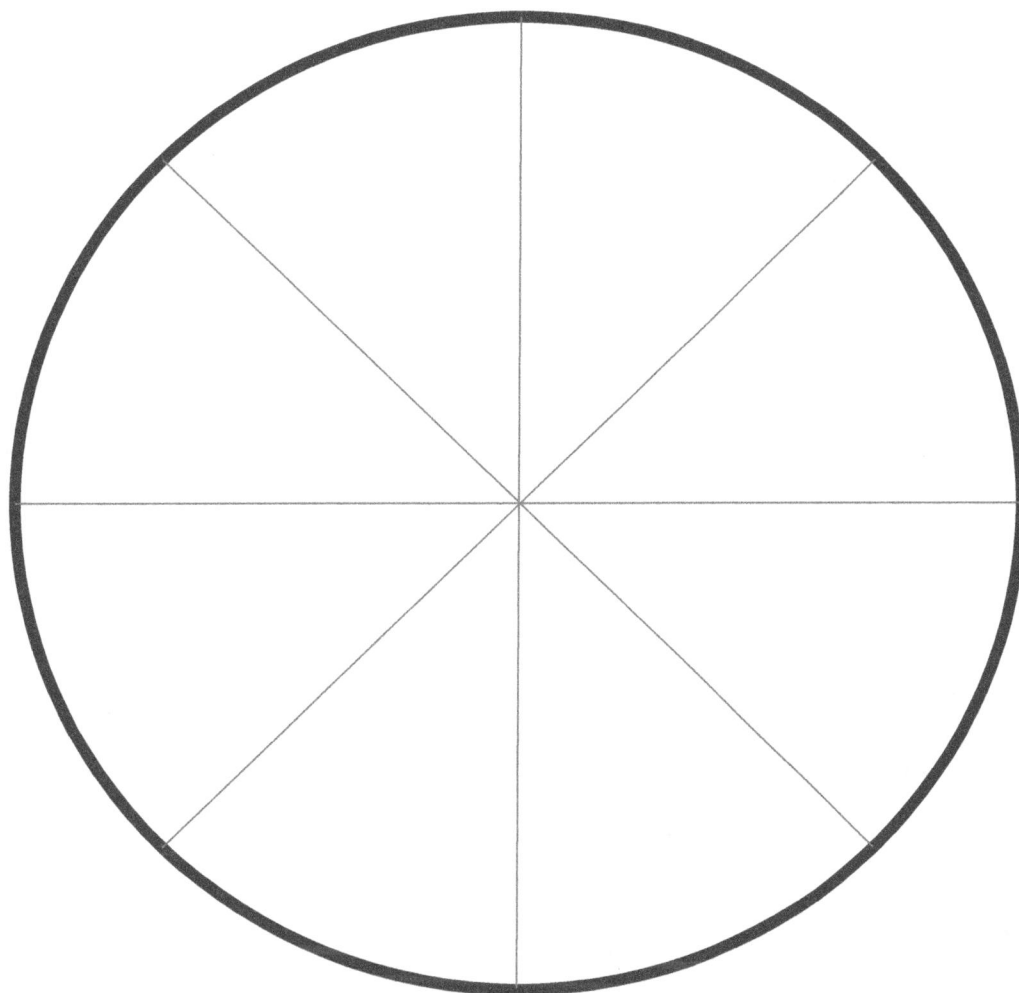

For each option, fill in the level of Benefit and the level of Risk.

Identify, visually, which is the best alternative.

The Consequences Chart

Desired / Best Case   **Worst Case**

Option 1

Option 2

Option 3

Effects on: _____

- Company
- Project Group
- Me
- Time
- Money
- Resources

Who Decides?

<u>Individual decision</u>

Who decides? _____

Why? _____

Expert advice from: _____

Input / discussion with: _____

Stakeholders are: _____

Communication to others from: _____

<u>Group decision</u>

Who decides? _____

Why? _____

Group consensus?   OR   Majority win?

Expert advice from: _____

Input / discussion with: _____

Stakeholders are: _____

Communication to others from:_____

Don't forget to consider the consequences of each choice!

Priority Chart

Assignments to be completed:

Project / Assignment	Time required	Due Date	Priority order

** This priority chart can be used for one person or for one multi-component project.

Assignment Chart

As much as we all want to remember who we delegated what to, when, and deadlines, it may not be possible.

Task	Assigned to	Start date	End date	Status Mtg frequency

** This chart can be sorted by Project, by Person, or by Date.

Decision Making

It's time Use Your B.R.A.I.N.!

Now it's time. You've learned what Decision Making is, how to use your B.R.A.I.N. and steps to decision making. You've also learned how decision making can vary based on who and what problems are at hand. You've even learned about other factors which influence your decisions. You've been given tools to assist you with your endeavors. Best of all, you've had a chance to get your feet wet by thinking about how to make decisions. These concepts can be applied both personally and professionally. Through the exercises in this book, you've had a chance to put the skills to work by practicing the techniques. You're ready to Use your B.R.A.I.N.!

Now it's time. Take what you have learned and put it to use. Start RIGHT NOW by jotting down at least 3 decisions that are best made right now, personally and professionally. Next, write down 3 more decisions that you can delay until later in the year. Finish up with noting 3 more decisions that are best left "pending" for the future. When you are done, you can tear out your list and tack it to your wall.

Now it's time to Use Your B.R.A.I.N.!

Decisions I will make now:

1.

2.

3.

Decisions I will intentionally delay until later:

Decisions for later this year (item and month):

1.

2.

3.

Decisions for next year:

1.

2.

3.

Tips for Successful Decision Making

1. Know your goal

2. Brainstorm the possibilities

3. Focus your energy

4. Do not over analyze

5. Look long term

6. Know the why (the reasons behind the basis)

7. Consider the costs – time, money, resources

8. Use "what if" scenarios

9. Remember, doing nothing is a choice

10. Act, don't re-act

11. Balance emotion with reason

12. Too many options leads to paralysis

13. Trust your intuition

14. Match the style to the situation (analytical, behavior, conceptual, directive)

15. Consider the consequences

16. Do a Cost : Benefit analysis

17. Adjust for assumptions

18. Start with the facts

19. Be aware of time constraints

20. Evaluate when complete

For More Information

Customized Caring, Inc.

901 Indigo Court
Hanover Park, Illinois 60133
www.CustomizedCaring.com

Contact Amy K. Atcha
at
630.306.4480
amy@customizedcaring.com

Life is precious. Take care of those you love.

www.ingramcontent.com/pod-product-compliance
Lightning Source LLC
LaVergne TN
LVHW081321060426
835509LV00015B/1625